Outside Play

Ruth Price

This book belongs to

....

HODDER
EDUCATION
AN HACHETTE UK COMPANY

Talk about the big photo.

Point to a pot. What colour is the pot? What are the children doing? What do you think they are making?

What else can you do with a pot?

Talk about the little photo.
What is in the pots? Food pots, flower pots… what other sorts of pot do you know? Can you say some words that rhyme with 'pot'?

Outside play
Outside play
What can you put
in a box today?

I can put bugs
in a box.

Talk about the big photo.
Point to the box. What is in it? What bugs would you like to put in the box? Where would you put the bugs back to keep them safe?

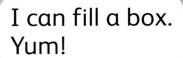

What else can you put in a box?

Talk about the little photo.

Say a word that rhymes with 'box'. Bug box, snack box… what other sorts of box do you know? What are these boxes made from?

Talk about the big photo.
Point to the bucket. What is in the bucket? What is he doing?
What is he mixing it with? What else could he use?

What else can you put in a bucket?

Talk about the little photo.
What is in the bucket? (shaving foam) How do you think it feels?
Clap the word 'bucket'. How many claps does it have?

Talk about the big photo.

Where are they? Point to a net. What are they trying to catch?
What do you like to catch in a net?

What else can you do with a net?

Talk about the little photo.
What sort of net is this? What is she doing? Have you climbed on a net?
Fishing net, climbing net… what other sorts of net do you know?

Talk about the big photo.

Point to the sack. What are the children doing? How do you think the children feel? Do you think it is easy to jump along in a sack?

What else can you do with a sack?

Talk about the little photo.

What are they doing? What will the sack help them to do?
Say a word that rhymes with 'sack'.

Outside play
Outside play
What can we do
in this pit today?

I can get
in a pit.

Talk about the big photo.

What sort of pit is it? Have you been in a pit like this?
How do the children feel and how do you know?

I can pat in a pit!

What else can you do in a pit?

Talk about the little photo.

What sort of pit is this? Sand pit, ball pit... what other sorts of pit do you know? What is another word for 'pit'?

Poems and rhymes

Outside

Time to play outside
The children cried.
We run all about
And scream and shout.
We run and hide
And scoot and ride.

We dance and sing
And jump on the swing.
We climb up the slide
And down we glide!
Quick! It looks like rain…
Let's do it all again!

By Ruth Price

Sing or say the poem.
Make your words glide when you say: 'And down we g-l-i-d-e!'
Find a rhyming word for: about, sing, rain.

Round and round

Round and round the
playground
Marching in a line.
I'll hold your hand
You hold mine.

Round and round the
playground
Skipping in a ring.
Everybody loves it
When we sing.

Round and round the
playground
That's what we like:
Climbing on the climbing
frame
Riding on the bike.

Round and round the
playground
All together friends.
We're sad, sad, sad
When the school day ends.

By John Kitching

Sing or say the poem.
Which five words are repeated in every verse?
Find a rhyming word for: line, ring, like.

Draw what you would put in each.

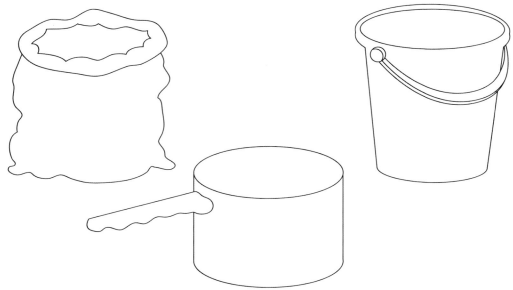

 Colour the pots red. Colour the buckets blue. Colour the sacks green. Colour the boxes yellow.